TODD TAYLOR'S
BANJO CHRISTMAS

Foreword by Joe Bonsall

ISBN 978-1-57424-321-5
SAN 683-8022

Cover by James Creative Group
Cover photo - Ken Marler
Notation - Paul Hinton

Special Thanks to
Dave & Chris - GHS Strings
Joe Carducci - Gretsch Company
Fred Gretsch - Gretsch Company
Gretchen Lee
Mike Moody

Todd Taylor plays Gretsch Banjos & Guitars
and GHS Banjo Strings

Copyright © 2015 CENTERSTREAM Publishing, LLC
P.O. Box 17878 - Anaheim Hills, CA 92817

www.centerstream-usa.com

Contents and CD Track List

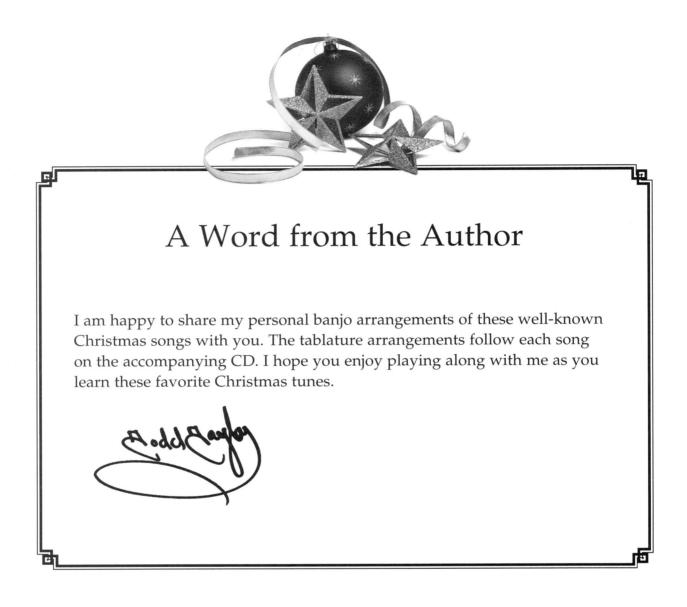

A Word from the Author

I am happy to share my personal banjo arrangements of these well-known Christmas songs with you. The tablature arrangements follow each song on the accompanying CD. I hope you enjoy playing along with me as you learn these favorite Christmas tunes.

About Todd Taylor

Todd "Banjoman" Taylor first fell in love with the banjo at just six years old. While on a family trip to Walt Disney World, Todd's parents realized he had wandered off. After a frantic search they found Todd on a steamboat ride -- mesmerized by the music of the banjo performer. His mom finally gave in to his pleadings and purchased his first banjo from a JCPenney catalog the following Christmas. Since then, Todd has enjoyed a music career spanning three decades.

As a teenager and young adult, he and his twin brother performed on the Grand Ole Opry with music legends Roy Acuff and Bill Monroe, and TV shows like *Live! With Regis and Kathy Lee*. Todd may be best known for using his unique style to elevate the banjo from the confines of bluegrass to build a bridge into all genres of music, especially rock 'n' roll. He was the first solo banjo musician featured on the *Rick Dees Weekly Top 40* internationally-syndicated radio program in the 1980's for his ground breaking arrangement and performance of Lynyrd Skynyrd's "Freebird."

Although Todd has donated his time to various worthwhile charities during his career, the Muscular Dystrophy Association (MDA) has a special place in his heart. In his twenties Todd became increasingly ill and almost lost his life. Extensive testing revealed he had inherited a mitochondrial disease, and despite his doctor's prognosis, Todd was determined to recover. He performed on the MDA telethon with Jerry Lewis on more than one occasion; increasing awareness of the disease and helping to raise funds for the organization's tireless efforts.

In 2007, Todd was the first to set the Guinness World Record for Fastest Banjo by performing both parts of "Dueling Banjos" at a mind-blowing 210 beats per minute! He dedicated his record to everyone fighting to overcome a disease or obstacle in their life, and continues to encourage others who may be struggling about the power of a positive attitude.

2011 produced Todd's rock 'n' blues tablature book, *Pickin' Over the Speed Limit*, and a feature in the documentary *Breaking and Entering*, highlighting his Guinness World Record achievement. He has earned dozens of Grammy nominations over the past decade in multiple categories, from original song composition to producing. Todd's eighth and latest CD, *Indescribable*, earned six Grammy nominations – most of them attributed to his performance of "Bach Cello Suite No. 1 in G Major," accompanied by Thornton Cline on cello and long-time friend Mike Moody on bass. But the pinnacle of his career came in 2012 when Governor Nikki Haley presented Todd with the Order of the Palmetto, the highest civilian honor in South Carolina, for his inspiring personal example and musical contribution to his home state. Todd says, "My life has been blessed in so many ways, and I have no plans to stop sharing the gift God has given me."

Foreword

As a banjo student I confess to needing all the help I can get. Like many who aspire to greater heights, we lean upon our banjo heroes for inspiration and learning. My hero is Todd Taylor. After years of admiring his work from afar I am honored now to call him a friend and a brother. He is not only the fastest banjo player in the world but he is among the most innovative musicians alive today. This book and CD are clear evidence of his immeasurable talent and teaching ability. Listen, read and learn from Todd and then at Christmastime amaze your family with some holiday banjo. Thank you Todd for all that you are and for all that you stand for. Congratulations on a great Hal Leonard project. It is EPIC my brother...

Joe Bonsall

42-year member of American music group The Oak Ridge Boys, author of ten books, and a half-baked banjo player.

Playing Tips about the Songs

Jingle Bells - When playing this song, play brightly with a lot of feeling.

Away In a Manger – I arranged this version in the key of G. When playing this song, play with a happy feeling. If you are playing along with the CD, the piano starts this version, then the banjo starts after the piano introduction.

Deck the Dueling Halls - Play this song with a lively feel. I arranged this version to challenge the guitar. The guitar starts, then you follow on the banjo.

Silent Night - Play this song slowly with lots of feeling. Page 2 will be all forward rolls, as the tabs indicate. If playing with the CD the strings are the intro to this song then banjo comes in.

What Child Is This - Play this song smoothly with plenty of feeling and once again if you play with the CD the piano intro will start the song then the banjo starts.

God Rest Ye Merry Gentlemen - Play semi-fast with authority. The banjo is in open G tuning. If you are playing along with the CD, the pipe organ starts the song then the banjo comes in after the organ introduction. Also, on the E minor parts, play with authority.

O Little Town of Bethlehem - Play this piece moderately with feeling. If playing with the CD, the banjo starts after the piano introduction.

We Wish You a Merry Christmas - Play this song very joyfully

O Christmas Tree - This song should be played moderately.

Good King Wenceslas - Play this song with a moderate, flowing feel - like a flowing stream.

Jingle Bells

G Tuning

Traditional - Arrangement by Todd Taylor

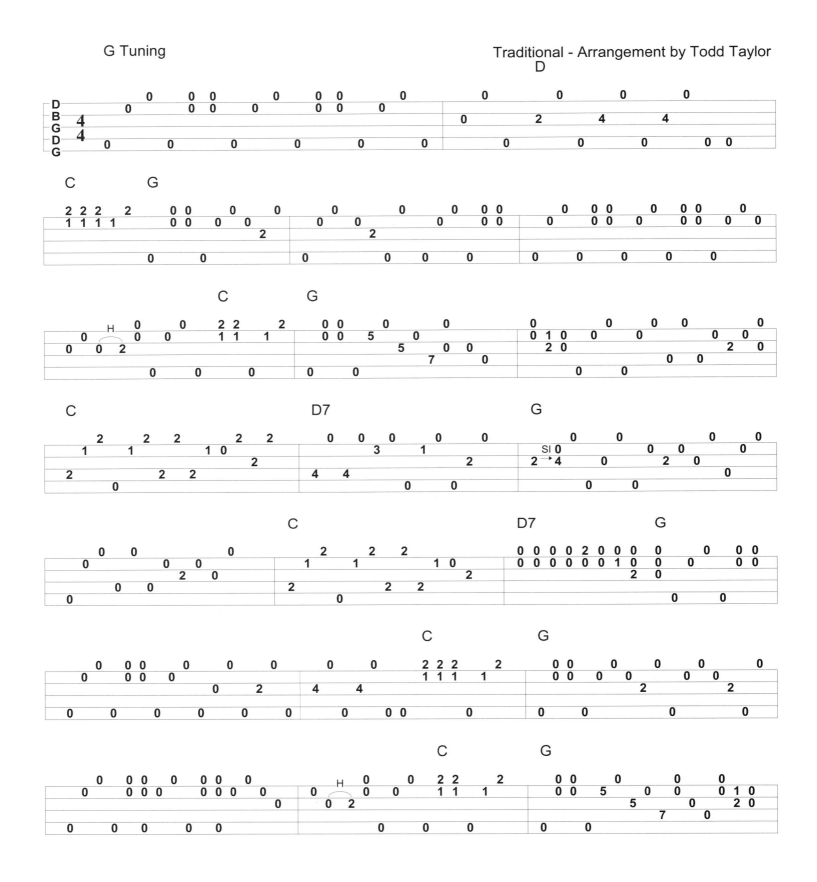

8

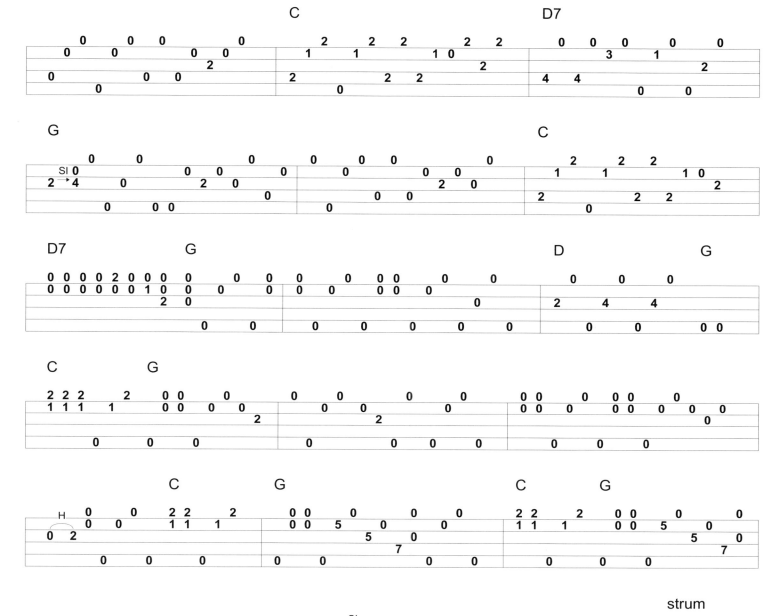

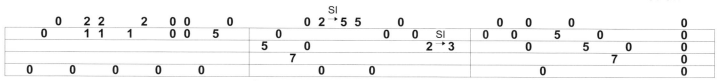

Away In a Manger

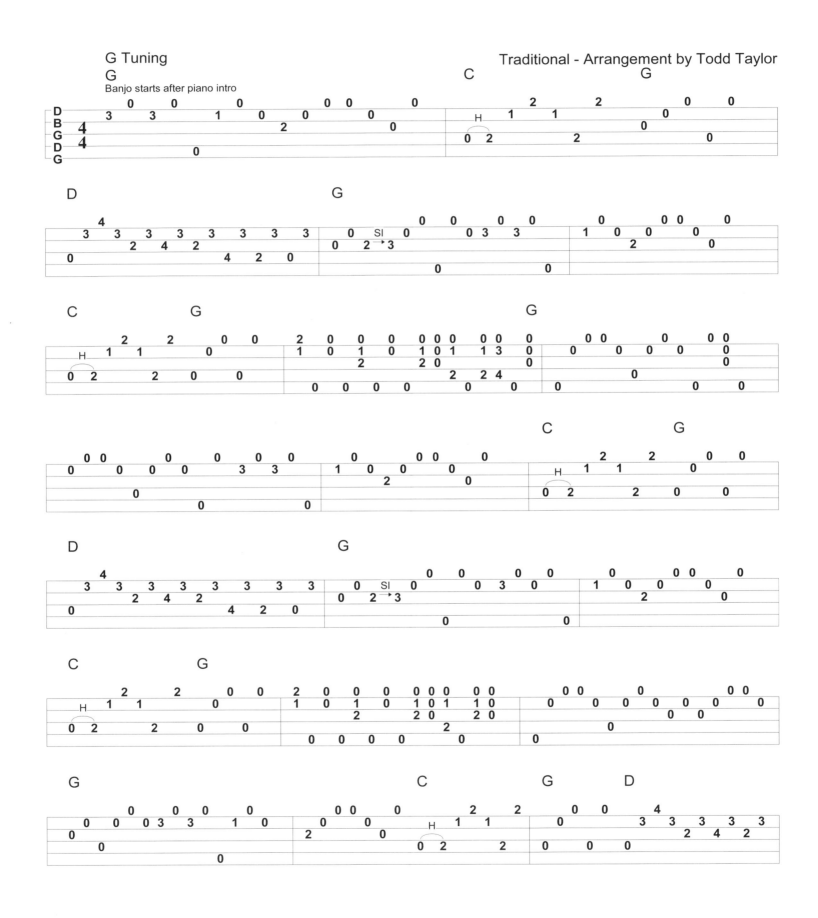

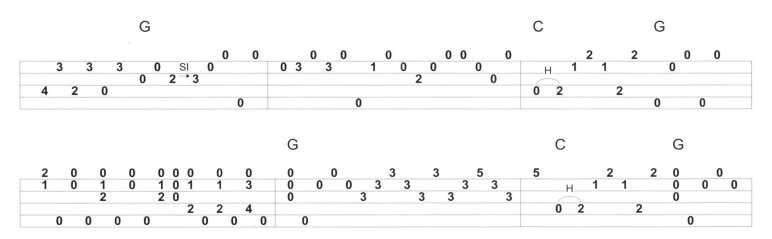

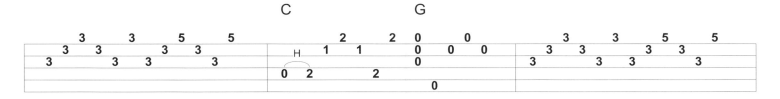

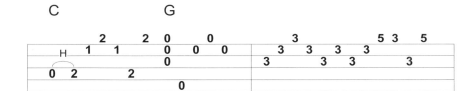

Deck the Dueling Halls

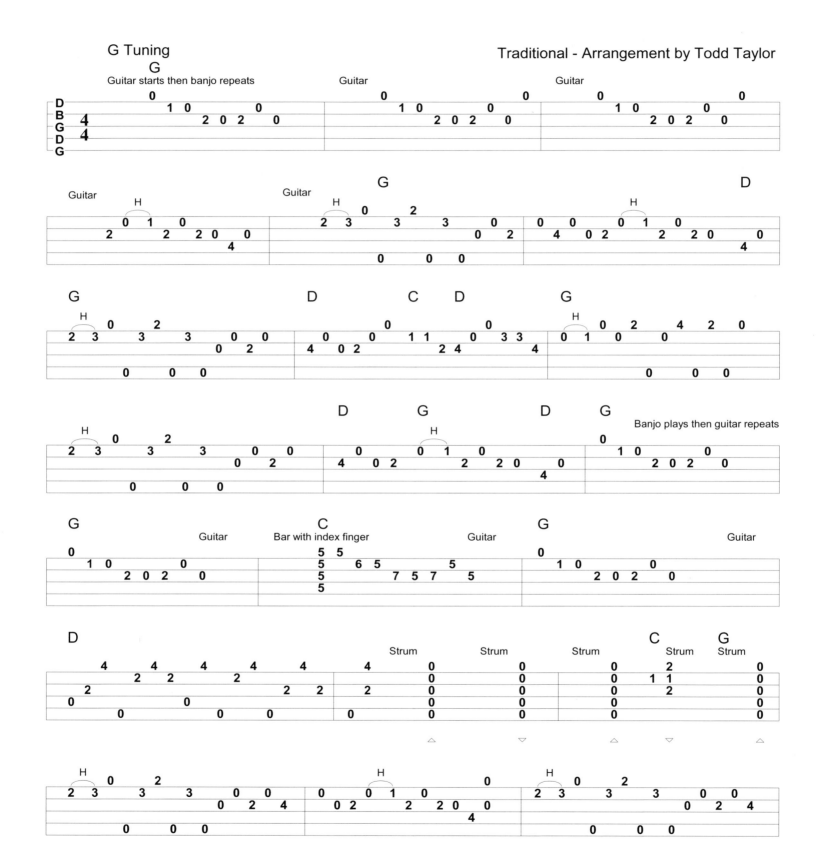

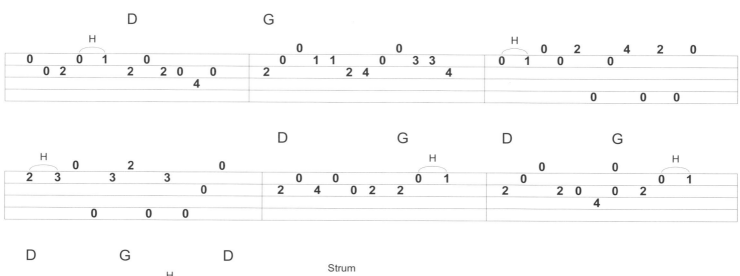

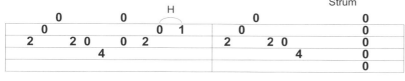

Todd Taylor and Joe Bonsall.

Silent Night

G Tuning

Traditional - Arrangement by Todd Taylor

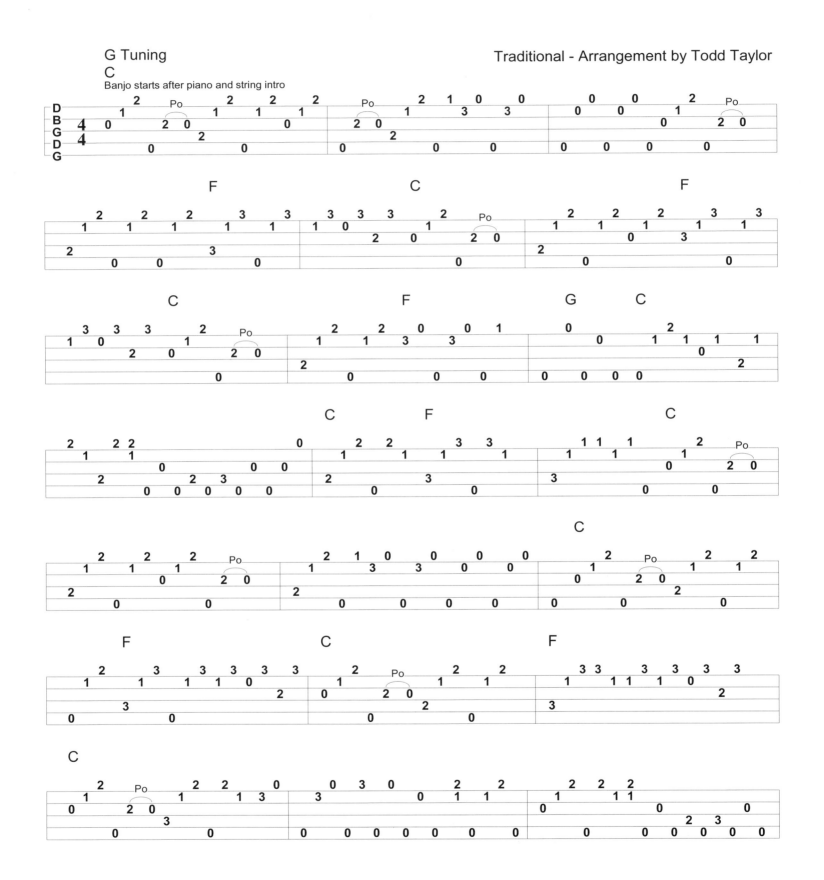

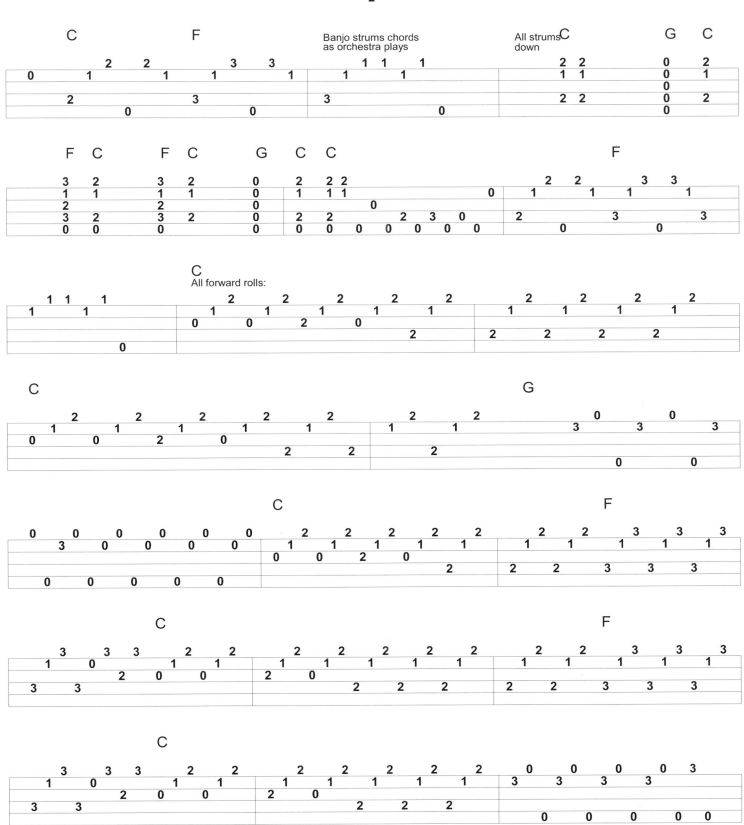

15

What Child Is This

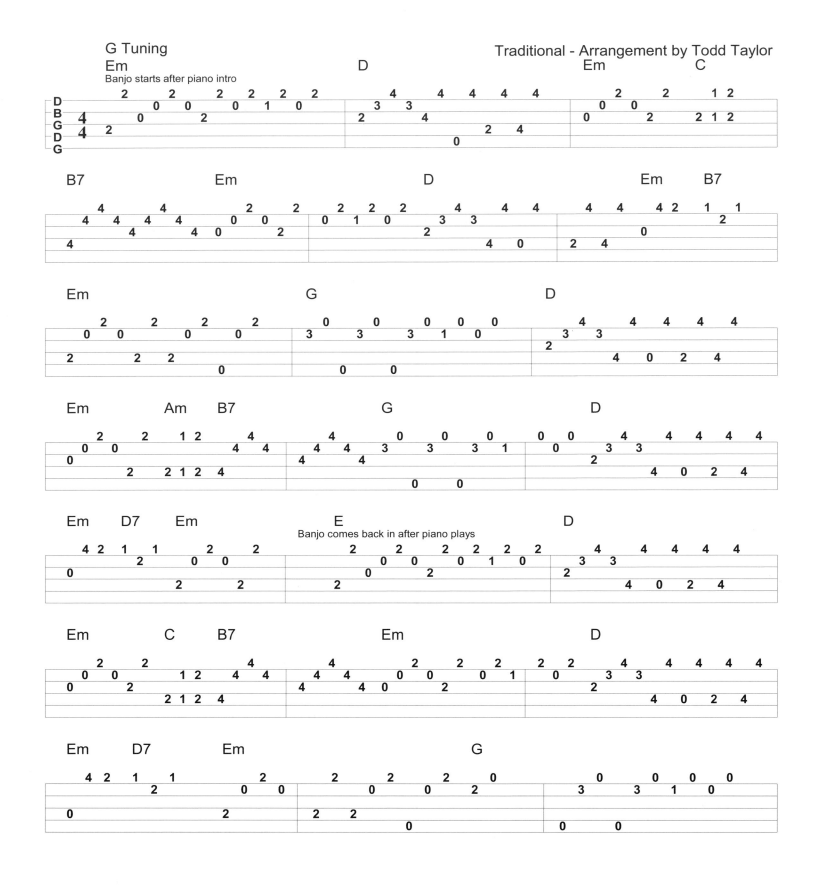

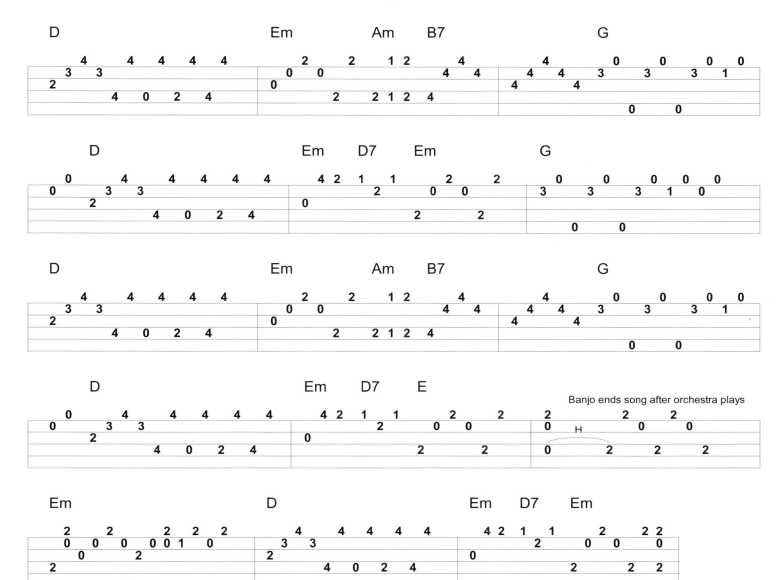

Banjo ends song after orchestra plays

God Rest Ye Merry Gentlemen

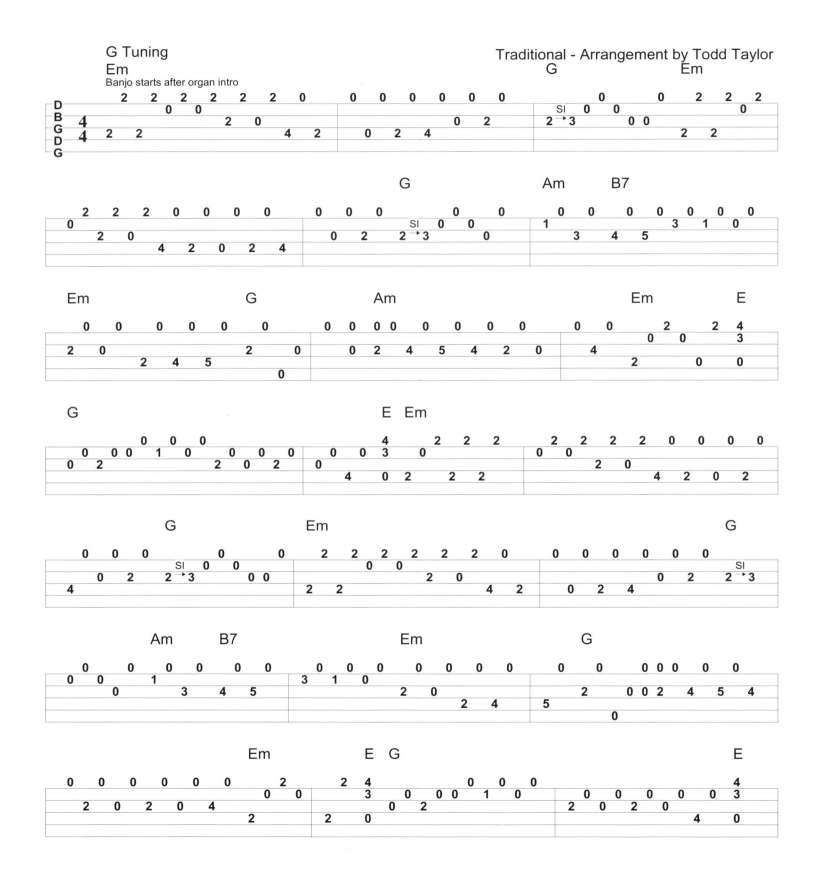

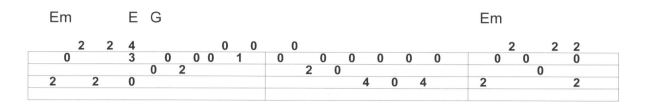

O Little Town of Bethlehem

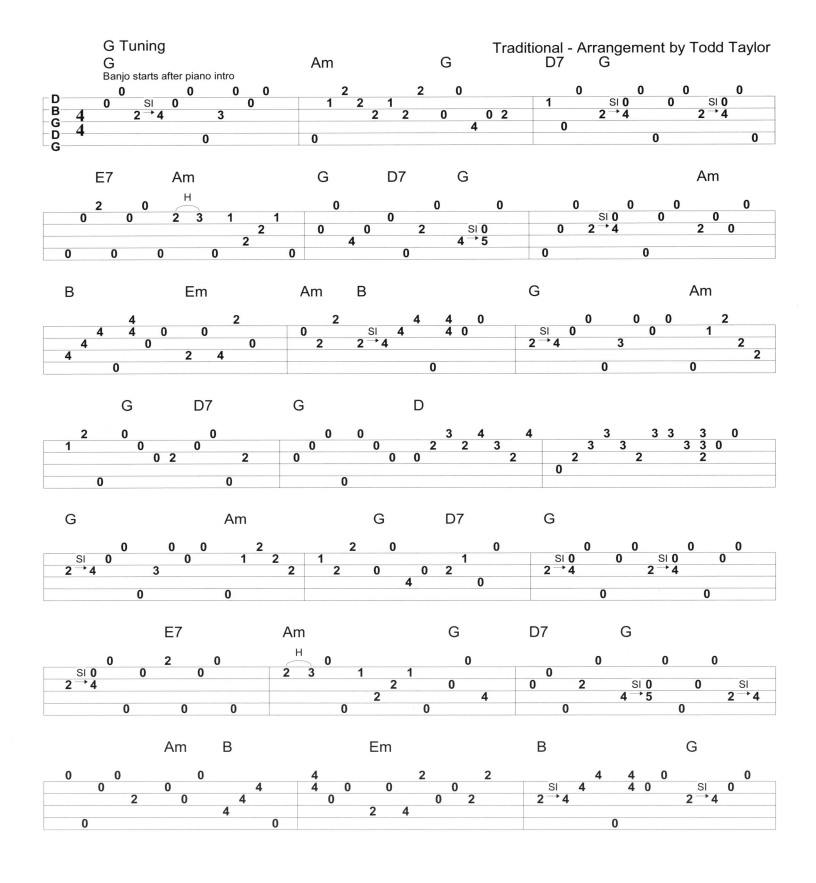

2

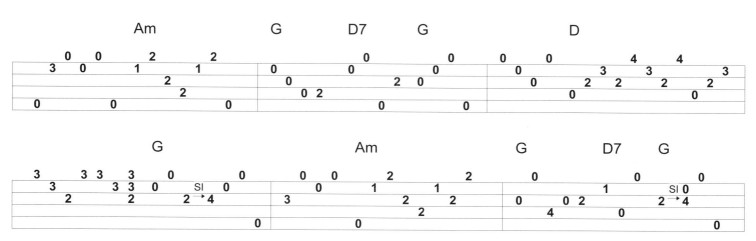

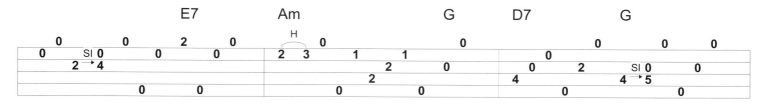

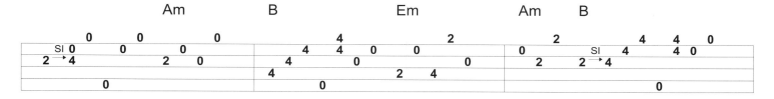

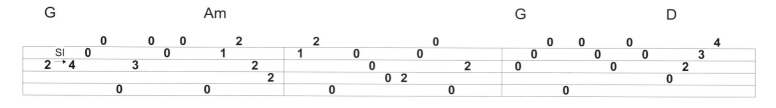

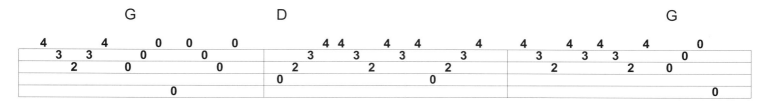

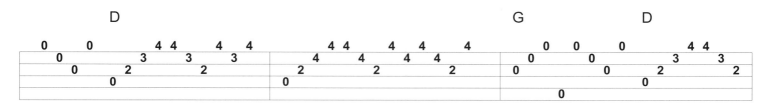

3

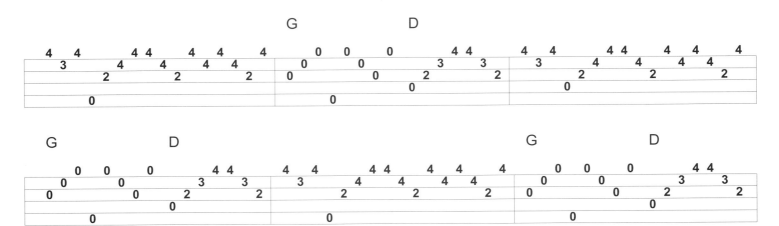

```
G                    D
    4   4        4 4     4   4       4               0   0       0           4 4       4   4       4 4     4   4       4
      3         4      4       4     4                 0         0       0         3     3         3       4         4     4     4     4
        2           2             2                      0         0           2           2             2       2         2         2
                                                            0                                 0
      0                                                   0
```

```
G                    D                                                          G                    D
      0   0       0           4 4                     4   4       4 4     4   4       4               0   0       0           4 4
    0         0       0           3     3             3       4         4     4     4                 0         0       0           3     3
        0         0           2           2             2         2         2                           0         0           2           2
                      0                                                                                     0
        0                                                   0                                               0
```

```
      4   4        4 4     4   4       4
        3         4      4       4     4
          2           2             2
            0
```

We Wish You a Merry Christmas

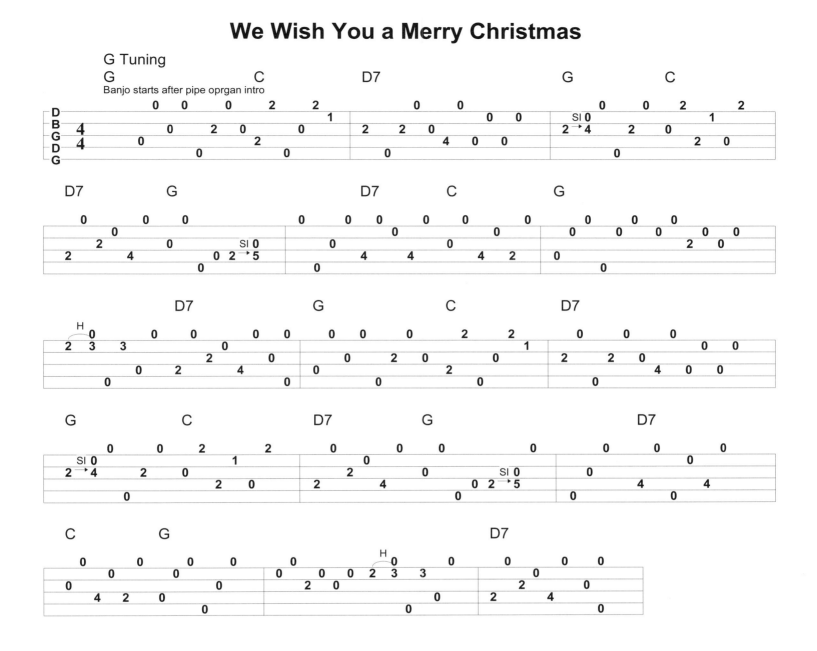

O Christmas Tree

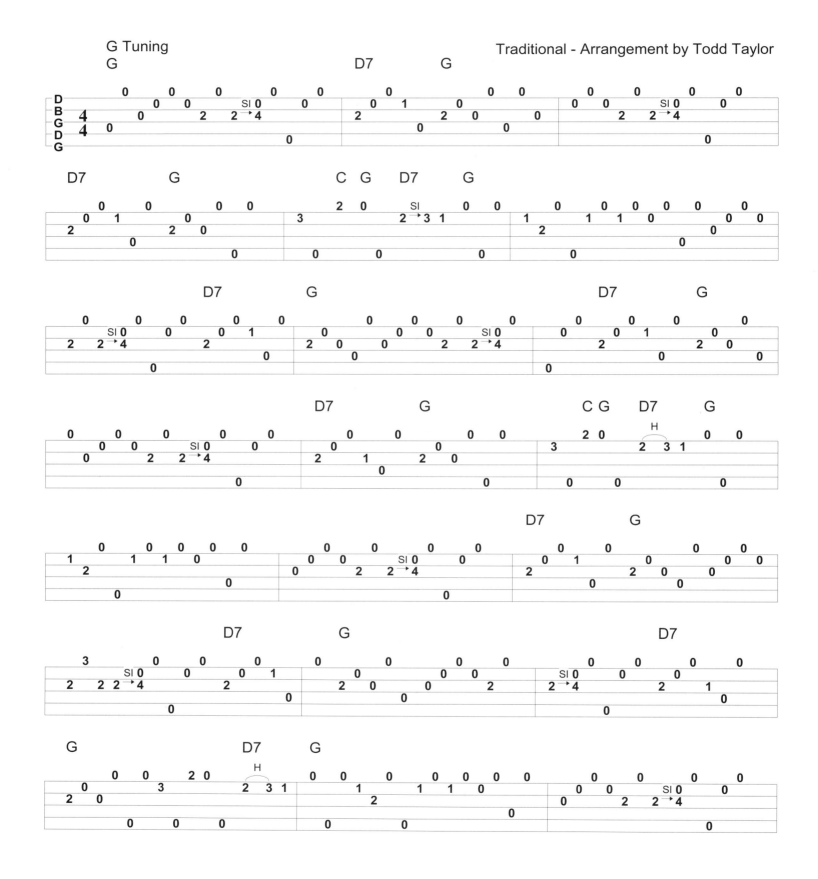

D7   G

```
        0    0                                          0
    0   1        0    0 1            0 1          0 1        0
2           2  0 2       0 2     2      0 2    2       0 2   0
    0                            4 0         4 0           4 0
                 0                    0            0
```

Fred Gretsch and Todd Taylor.

Good King Wenceslas

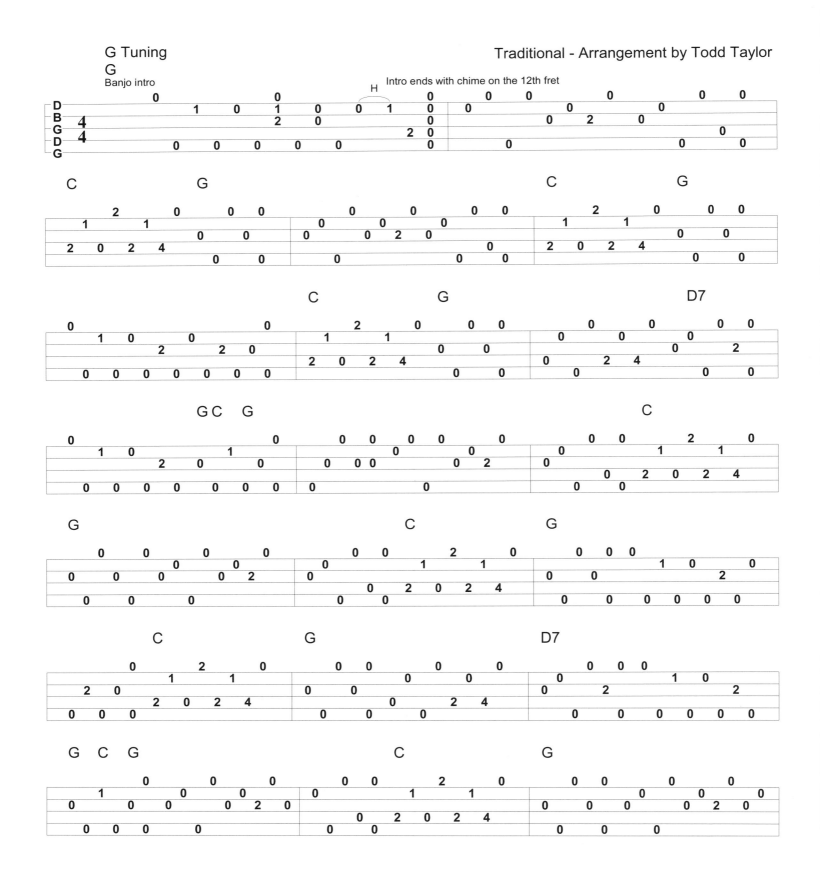

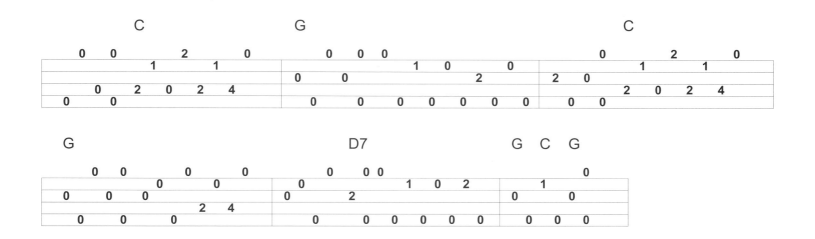

More Great Banjo Books from Centerstream...

28